# Blockchain Beginners Bible:

*Discover How Blockchain Could Enrich Your Life, Your Business & Your Cryptocurrency Wallet*

*By Stephen Satoshi*

# Table of Contents

Additionally, the information in the following pages is intended only for informational purposes and should thus be thought of as universal. As befitting its nature, it is presented without assurance regarding its prolonged validity or interim quality. Trademarks that are mentioned are done without written consent and can in no way be considered an endorsement from the trademark holder.

**Financial Disclaimer:**

I am not a financial advisor, this is not financial advice. This is not an investment guide nor investment advice. I am not recommending you buy any of the coins listed here. Any form of investment or trading is liable to lose you money.

There is no single "best" investment to be made, in cryptocurrencies or otherwise. Anyone telling you so is deceiving you.

There is no "surefire coin" - one again, anyone telling you so is deceiving you.

With many coins, especially the smaller ones, the market is liable to the spread of misinformation.

Never invest more than you are willing to lose. Cryptocurrency is not a get rich quick scheme.

# Introduction

Hi, I'm Stephen and I'm a blockchain addict.

Well, enthusiast is probably a better term - although I still definitely check my cryptocurrency portfolio far too frequently.

I've certainly come a long way from the young man who first heard about this Bitcoin thing back in the 2010s. You know, that new internet currency that people were making money from.

How could a currency be worth anything if it isn't backed by a central government? Oh, how naive I was.

This initial exposure to Bitcoin sparked an interest in blockchain technology and it's potential. I try to refrain from hyperbole but I truly believe this is mankind's greatest invention since Tim Berners-Lee invented the world wide web back in 1989.

You see, although Bitcoin and cryptocurrency in general is a large part of the blockchain movement, it goes beyond that.

There are serious political, social and economic ramifications that will come as a result of decentralization. An incorruptible permanent record, accessible by the masses, has a myriad of uses that can undoubtedly benefit society as a whole.

If you're reading this book, you're mostly likely a skeptic of big government, and you have every right to be. As recently as 2016, we witnessed a United States General Election in which both sides accused the other of vote tampering, in what is supposedly the world's leading democracy.

In short, governance as we know it has to be questioned.

Blockchain technology allows for indisputable trust on a level such as this. Banks, governments, hospitals, all the way down to small one-man-operation businesses can benefit.

That is the true future of this technology.

I hope this is just the start of your blockchain journey, and I hope it not only makes you a lot of money, I hope it enriches the quality of your life.

One final thing, if you enjoy this book I'd appreciate it if you took 2 minutes to leave it a review on Amazon.

Thanks,
Stephen

# Chapter 1: What is Blockchain Technology?

Over the past few years, you have likely heard more and more people talking about cryptocurrency this, or blockchain that. If you don't understand these terms, don't worry, you aren't alone. It may be time to jump on the bandwagon, however, as blockchain use is rapidly approaching consumer status with IBM estimating that 15 percent of banks will already be using blockchain technology by the end of 2017.

Simply put, blockchain is the foundation that makes technologies like cryptocurrency possible. On a fundamental level, a blockchain takes data, primarily of financial nature for now, and replicates that data across a vast number of decentralized nodes that could conceivably be spread around the entire world. This process is run not by a centralized network or body, but by a peer-to-peer approach that uses cryptography and digital signatures to keep things running smoothly.

Each new block in a chain contains information regarding various transactions, and possibly what are known as smart contracts, as well as information that links it to the blocks around it. Each block is also timestamped which helps the chain determine its place in the whole thing. The transactions in individual blocks are verified by block miners, third parties who are paid for their work, and are only then added to the chain as a whole.

What miners are actually doing is solving what are known as proof-of-work systems which means they are solving complicated mathematical equations using specialized equipment designed for doing so. The equations prevent security breaches through denial of service attacks and keep things running smoothly. The amount of reward for this type of work varies based on the cryptocurrency that is being mined, as well as the number of people working to complete the block they were chosen to mine. Most cryptocurrencies also charge a small transaction fee, and a part of that fee goes to the miners as well.

Despite the fact that the database information is spread around the world with no central authority, and the fact that sections of it are inspected by third parties on a regular basis, the data that is stored in a blockchain remains incredibly secure. This level of security doesn't come from an active offense against fraud, it comes from the defensive capabilities of the way in which the blockchain is constructed.

If a specific transaction that is being transferred from a node doesn't match up with what the other nodes are saying then that block is discarded in favor of a more accurate one. Essentially, for a false block to make it past the blockchain's defenses, it would need to show up on 51 percent of all of the nodes in the system at the same time. The difficulty of such a task means that it could be done, but the costs involved would more than outweigh the potential reward for doing so.

## History lesson

In order to understand the true importance of blockchain technology, it is helpful to understand a little bit about its history. In 2008, a person or a group of persons using the alias Satoshi Nakamoto put forth a whitepaper on the idea of a digital currency that would allow individuals to transfer money to one another in a largely anonymous fashion. This paper, titled, *bitcoin: A Peer-to Peer Electronic Cash System,* was soon followed by the original blockchain and bitcoin code from the same alias. The code was released in an open source fashion, and the Nakamoto name faded from sight as other developers began working on the code in earnest.

The Nakamoto alias was also the first person to distribute bitcoins and then verify the transaction, receiving 50 bitcoins for doing so. For those who are considering investing in a cryptocurrency based on blockchain technology, take note, as the first use of those bitcoins was to trade 10,000 of them for a pair of large pizzas which made each worth about $.002. If you weren't aware, they are doing a little better than that these days with each bitcoin being worth nearly $5,000 as of September 2017.

By 2014, blockchain usage was gaining some traction and a new and improved version of the original code now allowed for entire programs to be contained in blocks along with data that make it possible for a wide variety of tasks to be carried out from within the blockchain. In 2016, the Russian Federation started working on a blockchain program as a means of collecting royalties for copyrighted material, making Russia the first country to official announce a blockchain project, though since that time a number of other countries, including China and the US, have indicated they are working on blockchain projects of their own. When the project was announced, the Russian Economic Minister was quoted as saying that blockchain technology was likely the most important new technology since the invention of the internet.

Over the past few years, another blockchain based company, the Ethereum platform has been gaining a lot of support due to its wide variety of enhanced capabilities when compared to the bitcoin blockchain. The Ethereum platform has its own official cryptocurrency, ether (although the two terms are used interchanably by many commentators), and is also home to an ecosystem of other cryptocurrencies that other programmers have made to run in its framework. It is also home to a wide variety of smart contracts and apps that run on "gas", which is essentially a transaction fee the platform collects for each transaction. Ether blocks that are mind tend to be completed in a shorter timeframe than bitcoin blocks and the Ethereum chain can handle a great many more blocks at a time when compared to the bitcoin chain.

*Database differences:* The biggest difference between a blockchain database and a traditional database is the level of centralization that is required in order for it to run effectively. Even if a traditional server is decentralized, the core components are going to be arranged as close to one another as possible to facilitate the transfer of information. Instead, blockchains are formed of nodes that are separated by thousands of miles, each communicating with the others through a best use model that means they naturally seek out the nodes that are closest to them and the information spreads out from there.

The fact that mass collaboration and the blockchain code results in a reliable means by which funds can be transferred is a game changer. Blockchain is the first innately digital medium where value can be transferred, in much the way the internet allowed for information to be transmitted digitally.

*Hashes:* A hash is a mathematical function that makes up a crucial part of the blockchain security matrix. This is the function that ensures the data that is added to a blockchain remains secure regardless of who might get their hands on it. The function encrypts the data in such a way that it becomes a fixed length output, which can be thought of as a type of digital fingerprint. When it comes to blockchain security the most commonly used hash function is SHA-256. SHA-256 is used by cryptocurrencies such as Bitcoin, Omni and Zetacoin.

The hash function for every block is going to be different, which means that if that data is altered by a malevolent third party then the entire fingerprint would be rearranged in unpredictable ways. Additional hash information is added once the block is added to the chain as a whole. This process is repeated throughout the blockchain each time a new block is added so that it is always changing.

*Merkle trees:* Hashes are then used by a process known as the Merkle tree which is a quick and easy way for the blockchain to verify all of its data once a new block has been added. Each hash is unique and created based on the data it contains which means the Merkle tree then essentially needs to scan the hash, compare it to the root hashes which is the ultimate collection of all the hashes, and then determine if everything lines up as it should. Each time it does this, it creates a pair of roots, one where the data is correct and one where it is not, this way it keeps the core details of the blockchain intact against malicious changes.

# Chapter 2: Practical Application of Blockchain Technology

As blockchain technology continues to grow in popularity, the ways in which it can be put to use are growing as well. What follows are a number of different ways blockchain technology is sure to change how business is conducted, day to day life, outside the realm of cryptocurrency and how governments and lawmakers interact with the public.

# Business uses

*Money transfers and payments:* While blockchain technology is already synonymous with cryptocurrency payments, the fact of the matter is that more can be done in that space to facilitate the needs of businesses when it comes to utilizing blockchain to its fullest potential. The Ethereum Enterprise Alliance is a group of major corporations such as Microsoft, JP Morgan and Samsung that are working together to build a blockchain that is based on Ethereum technology but also contains the level of control that businesses would need in order to use the technology on a regular basis.

This type of service, while extremely common in some parts of the world, are extremely hard to come by in others. As such, more people in Kenya currently have a bitcoin wallet than have indoor plumbing. Connecting all these new individuals to the internet is going to have serious positive ramifications for retailers worldwide.

*Notary services:* Blockchain technology is constructed in such a way that it could conceivably be used to replace traditional notary services. There are already numerous different apps available that allow for notarization of a variety of different types of content.

*Cloud storage:* Blockchain technology is already being used as a means of connecting users with cloud storage space in an Airbnb like setup. Using this system those with spare storage space on their hard drives can rent out the extra space to those who are in need of extra storage. The estimate is that worldwide spending has reached more than $20 billion for cloud storage so this could be a profitable opportunity if this catches on.

*Fraud:* Blockchain technology has the potential to increase the efficacy of tracking identities online in a way that is both efficient and secure. Blockchain is uniquely situated to solve this problem because its results are sure to be properly authenticated, immutable, secure and irrefutable. This improved system will do away with complicated password or dual factor authentication systems in favor of a system that will ultimately use digital signatures and cryptography to keep everyone safe and efficiently catalogued.

Using this type of system, the transaction will be processed as normal, and the only check that will be required is if the account from which the funds are drawn, matches the account of the person who authorized the transaction. A variation of this same usage of the technology can also be used when it comes to birth certificates, passports, residency forms, account logins and physical identification. There are already apps available that utilize a blockchain to verify the identity of users from a mobile device.

*Supply chain communication:* If it is one thing that companies have a hard time dealing with, it is the extreme level of communication that is required in order to ensure that they have all the requirements at the ready to ensure they are ready to do whatever it is they do. Blockchain technology allows for companies to easily track products from door to door, with the internet of things (the ability for everyday objects to send and receive data) connecting shipping containers to accounts that get a steady stream of details about the product in question as it crosses various thresholds and ultimately automatically pays for the goods once they have reached their final location. SkuChain and Provenance are two companies that are working to create these types of systems.

*Gift cards:* Gift cards are a good idea in theory that ultimately falls apart in practice when it comes time for the customer to actually hold onto the card in question. Blockchain technology has the potential to change all that by connecting customer loyalty products directly to a blockchain which can then verify and update relevant information as needed. Gyft Block is a company that already has a digital gift card up and running on the bitcoin blockchain that can be traded just like a cryptocurrency.

*Internet of things:* Samsung and IBM are currently working together on a concept referred to as the Autonomous Decentralized Peer-to-Peer Telemetry or ADEPT, which uses blockchain as a means of creating a system that mixes proof of stake and proof of work systems to better secure transactions. Essentially, what they are trying to do is to create a blockchain that would act like a public ledger for a wide number of devices. This public ledger would then serve as a hub which can create a bridge between devices for a very low cost. These devices could then communicate with one another in a practically autonomous fashion, making it easy to save energy, sort out bugs and issue updates.

*Insurance contracts:* Smart contracts have the possibility to reinvent insurance in a big way. Rather than deal with insurance agents who have to determine liability in case of a business-related injury, a blockchain would be able to make use of a smart contract that issues payments if a specific interconnected item registers a faulty signal. Blockchain would then allow for a more streamlined claim process that would improve the customer experience and ultimately save the company money.

*Funding:* 4G Capital is a company that provides access to credit for small businesses in Africa through the use of a decentralized app that is running off of the Ethereum blockchain. Donors are able to use the app to spend their cryptocurrency funds directly to the recipient of their choice. The money is then converted to the currency of the applicant and dispersed using a proprietary transaction system. In addition to providing 100 percent unsecured loans to those who often would not be able to get them otherwise, it also provides business training and consulting services. While currently operating in a limited capacity, if it proves successful more operations offering this type of funding are sure to appear.

*Microblogging:* Businesses are always looking for new ways to interact with their target audience and blockchain may be the next new frontier. Projects like Eth-Tweet offer decentralized microblogging services through the Ethereum blockchain. The service operates much like Twitter, except that as a truly decentralized entity there is no one who can pressure users to take content down and no one can remove messages after they have been added to the chain.

# Day to Day Life

*Healthcare:* Real world tests are already being done that link individuals to their healthcare status as they are going through a hospital. Early studies from the MIT Media Lab show that this practice can decrease errors by up to 30 percent in nonemergency situations. This is a huge step forward for hospitals that are often not designed for the volume and range of data that is being created these days. Patient data can even continue to be gathered on an outpatient basis or if the individual has agreed to be part of a test group. Payment for these tests could then be issued automatically once the required data has been successfully gathered.

*Internet decentralization:* With the rise of Google, the internet is a much more centralized place than it once was. A startup by the name of Blockstack is working to change all of that. It is on track to release prototype software in the second half of 2017 which will make it possible for anyone to utilize blockchain technology to access a version of the internet where you have much more control over your personal data. This decentralized internet will act the same way the traditional internet does, except that instead of creating a different account for every website, the process will reverse and you will create a primary account, then give certain sites access to it.

If you are then finished using a specific site you can then completely revoke its access to your data at any time. While this might seem like a small step, it is actually a giant leap for a new and improved internet. Blockstack makes use of a digital ledger to track usernames and various levels of encryption, with the end result being a greater degree of privacy control for the individual user. The blockchain will also keep track of domain names as well, potentially making ICANN, the web domain oversight body, obsolete. Microsoft is already in talks with Blockstack to make use of its technology.

While the way it handles web functions might seem extreme, it is actually the low-level features of the internet as a whole that have led to the dominance of corporations who essentially have free reign to treat user data as they see fit. The new platform will still offer companies ways to make money while providing services, the balance of power is just going to favor the consumer more than it does now.

*Improved property rights:* Both tangible and intangible property from cars and houses on one hand to company shares and patents on the other, can all be connected via smart contract and blockchain technology to make determining the rights to these items much less complicated than it currently is. These details could be stored in a type of decentralized ledger along with related contractual details regarding the true ownership of the property in question. The technology could even extend to smart keys which could then give specific users access to specific property.

The ledger would keep track of the finer details and activate specific keys as needed. In this case the decentralized ledger is also a system for managing and recording property rights and also creating duplicates if smart keys are lost. Implementing smart property protocols will help to decrease the average property owner's risk of fraud, questionable business deals and mediation fees.

*New types of money lenders:* With blockchain technology making it easier and easier to transfer funds between individuals, new types of hard money lenders are already popping up to take advantage of the fact. Hard money lenders are more likely to offer terms to individuals who already have subpar credit, unfortunately the terms are often quite high and often property is listed as collateral. This, in turn, causes many debtors to default on loans, and leaves them in a worse position than they were in initially. Lending via blockchain technology has the potential to change all of that as the binding nature of the transaction means that less collateral will be required and smart contracts can take care of the transactions themselves so costs will be decreased as well.

*Smarter smartphones:* Smartphones already operate on a type of cryptography in that they require either your fingerprint, a scan of your face, or a password in order to activate them. This is already a form of smart property, just in its nascent stages. This facet of personal technology will be enhanced via blockchain technology in that, rather than having these details tied to your physical SIM card, they will be stored in the blockchain where you can easily access them no matter where you are. While issues concerning security would typically arise in these sorts of situations, the fact that each transaction needs to be verified in order to add it to the chain ensures security remains tight.

*Passports:* Blockchains have been helping people manage their passports since at least 2014 by making it easier for users to identify themselves regardless if they are online or offline. This system works by taking a picture of the user and encoding it with a private key as well as a public one. The passport is then stored in a public ledger which can be accessed via a blockchain address by the person who has the key.

*Important documents:* It doesn't matter if it is a wedding certificate, birth certificate or death certificate, all of these documents confer various rights or privileges. This would be less of an issue if it weren't for the fact that the physical systems that keep track of these details are prone to mistakes. In fact, according to UNICEF, as many as 30 percent of all children who are below the age of five do not have a birth certificate. Implementing a public blockchain to streamline this process would not only make keeping track of these services more manageable, it will make these documents easier to obtain as well.

*Identification:* Currently you have to carry your driver's license, your work identification card, your social security card, the list goes on and on. With the right blockchain, however, all of this could be a thing of the past. Eventually everyone is going to have a digital ID that goes with them everywhere. It will be connected to a worldwide protected ledger and it will contain all the basic details you now need to carry around with you.

*Improve digital interactions:* With a wider and wider variety of interactions being initiated online, it is often difficult to know whom you can trust. Blockchain can alleviate that problem by storing a version of your identity in a blockchain that is available for everyone to see. It would automatically pull in things like review scores and rankings from a wide variety of sites so you always have at least a general idea of what you are in for before taking an online interaction into the real world. Unlike with more traditional types of social media, users would not have the ability to remove their information and start fresh, once it is in the blockchain it would be there forever.

*Change the way you fuel your vehicle:* Modern electric vehicles have already made great strides when it comes to the fueling process. Another important stride is on the horizon and it has to do with blockchain. Soon blockchain technology will be able to track the electricity that a given owner uses and automatically deduct the funds from the relevant account. All the owner would need to do is pull up to the charging station, the blockchain will take care of the rest.

# Beyond Cryptocurrency

*Fund HIV research:* The UBS bank recently donated a platform to Finclusion systems that will launch a smart contract called HealBond which will seek out efficient trades on the bonds market so that the funds that it makes can ultimately be put to use for HIV research. Analysts are confident that with the right level of passive strategy it could start making money right away. If this proves successful then it will give those with the resources to do so even more ways to help out their favorite causes.

*Data security:* The company Factom is turning its focus to properly securing data. Currently it is working with the country of Honduras to more accurately register land and also with a number of cities in China on what are known as Smart Cities. Blockchain technology is looking to an integral tool in getting all the various different systems communicating with one another on the same level. This includes things like data notarization services as well as information management with a much higher level of integrity than what is currently available to the public. Factom has also already received funding from the US Department of Homeland Security, specifically the Technology and Science Directorate to work on the Blockchain Software to Prove Integrity of Captured Data project.

*Decentralize the power grid:* Rather than requiring a centralized power provider that is in charge of sending energy to workplaces and homes, a decentralized blockchain could be built to allow people to generate power through solar and other means and then sell what they don't need on an open market. All of these transactions would then be visible on the blockchain, keeping fraud to a minimum. As more and more individuals are purchasing high-capacity batteries along with solar panels for their rooftops, this type of scenario is fast becoming a realistic possibility.

*Track things that are difficult to track:* The fact that a blockchain can show up at any time and cannot be altered makes it uniquely qualified to track the types of items that always seem to go missing. For example, the company Everledger is currently working on a way to identify specific objects and then determine whether or not they are legitimate. So far, they have created a distributed ledger that follows various diamond transaction verifications including law enforcement agencies, claimants, insurance companies and owners to put together a mine to store view of each diamond. The system is useful in that it keeps the supply chain honest and also makes it easier for individual buyers to determine if a given diamond is right for them. Furthermore, smart contracts make it possible for the diamond transactions to clearly be paid for while also tracking them, guaranteeing to consumers that they are not purchasing blood diamonds.

*Getting artists what they deserve:* Rather than having to worry about making sure their music isn't used without generating compensation, with blockchain, musicians will soon be able to determine who used each song and for what, with each individual transaction being carried out via smart contracts through a blockchain platform. What's more, rather than having to wait for funds to hit a specific level, or for someone, somewhere, to cut a check, these funds would be distributed in relatively real time. This same process can be applied to music licensing as a whole which means it will eventually be possible to cut out middlemen from the equation entirely. This, in turn, means a decrease in costs to the consumer and an increase in profit for the musicians as it means people are more likely to pay for content again.

*Improved communication:* Currently if your vehicle receives a safety recall then the maker of the vehicle sends out a notice to all of its licensed sales outlets and each of these outlets then reaches out to its customers who have purchased the vehicle in question. This information then may or may not reach you, allowing you to then make an informed decision based on the details you have available to you. The recall could be for something major, or something inconsequential, but regardless you are certainly going to want to know about it. Placing all of this information onto a blockchain would dramatically simplify the process as after the defect was found, the chain could automatically notify the owners in question.

*Clarifying asset lifecycles:* It doesn't matter who you are or what you do, you have certain tools that make your life possible. Blockchain technology has the ability to make sure you know as much about them as you need to when combined with the internet of things. Asset lifecycle is important for everyone from home business owners to multinational corporations, and the information provided by this type of blockchain could literally save lives. For example, think about an airplane which is likely to have several different owners during its time in the air. This type of blockchain would make it possible for every owner to understand every part on their airplane more completely and to ensure that proper maintenance has been completed throughout its lifetime.

*Tracking the food chain:* An increase in the ready availability of blockchain technology means that slowly but surely concerns about the quality of the food that you consume on a regular basis will be put to rest. Regardless of the final state of the product when you purchase it, you should be able to see the entire route it took to get to your table. Not just the completed product either, everything that went into the construction of the completed whole. This is particularly useful as there may be more to the traditional food chain than you might first realize. For example, a farm could produce vegetables that head to a processing facility before ending up in a distribution center before being purchased and run through another processing facility, all to end up in a can of tomato soup.

*Change the value of ownership:* The company Slock.it is based on the Ethereum platform and runs a blockchain for what is known as the Universal Share Network, this network is an opensource marketplace where anyone can go to list their unused asset, regardless if it is machinery, shipping containers, office space and more. It is a sort of automated AirBnB that works for anything and everything, not just temporary living arrangements. The fundamentals of blockchain technology are then passed on to tangible, real world assets.

*Transportation:* A variation in the trend towards the crowdsourcing of ridesharing applications, La'Zooz is a decentralized transportation platform that is owned by its users who use blockchain technology to organize and optimize a variety of smart transportation solutions.

# Government and lawmakers

Everywhere around the world, government organizations are rapidly exploring the many possibilities provided by blockchain and distributed ledger technology. The ability to suddenly be able to record and distribute ledger information easily and securely has created a market for a variety of new governmental approaches when it comes to establishing trust, preventing fraud and improving transparency.

From a recent survey from the Economic Intelligence Unit as well as IBM, it is clear that the interest in blockchain technology from various worldwide governments is quite high. In fact, as many as 9 out of 10 government agencies are already planning on investing in blockchain based contract management, asset management, regulatory compliance and transaction management by 2018. Meanwhile 7 of the 10 predict blockchain is going to significantly change the way that contract management is handled. Finally, nearly 20 percent say that they expect to have a blockchain plan up and running before the end of 2017.

*Voting:* As recently as the 2016 United States general election, both Republicans and Democrats could be heard questioning the security of the existing voting system. Likewise, the 2000 presidential election proved that the way that votes are tallied is remarkably out of date. While concerns about hacking have limited the acceptance of electronic means of voting so far, blockchain technology could easily put those fears to rest. A decentralized public ledger would naturally be encrypted but specific individuals could still confirm their votes were counted accurately. This system would not only be more efficient, but it would be more cost effective, and clearly more secure as well.

*Responsive, open data:* The blockchain ledger would also create a platform for what is known as responsive, open data. Studies show that this type of freely accessible data is likely to bring in nearly $3 trillion worldwide within the first year. Startups will be able to utilize this data to help get ahead of fraudulent activity, parents would be able to access details about the medications their children are receiving, the list is literally endless. Currently, this type of data is only available via limited, government approved windows which are not designed to put citizens first. As a blockchain is a type of public ledger, citizens would be able to access its data at any time and place.

*Self-management:* Blockchain provides the opportunity for governmental agencies to self-manage more easily as the exchange of information on a global scale would be greatly improved overall. There would be a great deal more trust as well because the information in the blockchain would be public for everyone to see.

*Reducing administration costs:* If property records were recorded to a blockchain then prospective buyers could more easily, quickly and cost effectively verify ownership information. This process is currently still done manually which means government agencies spend hundreds of thousands of dollars per year paying individuals who do this type of job. Manually verifying such things can also lead to an increased number of errors which helps to further increase potential costs.

It would also greatly decrease the amount of manual effort which would be required on the banks' end as they would have to do much less work when it comes to title insurance. Title insurance is required by lenders as a means to protect their interests. This, in turn, would decrease prices for homebuyers who are refinancing or buying for the first time because they would have to pay less throughout the entire process as the amount of labor would be reduced significantly.

*Decrease money laundering:* If identity data was readily store on a blockchain, the government agencies could more easily keep track of those who are moving large amounts of money from one place to another. Financial organizations could scan the details of every new client and that information could then be passed along to appropriate agencies if a need presented itself. Furthermore, storing payment and account information in a blockchain would go a long way to standardize the type of information required for an account. This, in turn, will help to improve the quality of the data that is gathered and reduce the number of legitimate transactions that are falsely listed as fraudulent. Finally, having a record that was known to be tamper-proof would make it easier for these organizations to comply with AML regulations.

*Ensuring taxpayers are paying up:* The Federal Government is likely already working on its own form of cryptocurrency, so there is no reason to assume they are not already working on a means of linking a blockchain to the current IRS system. This blockchain would not only record the amount of money each citizen earned in a year but also any incentives, subsidies, grants and loans that individual might have been provided with as well as there original source. While this will likely lead to more individuals having to pay more in taxes than they are currently, it will also keep the government accountable for every dime that they bring in. It will be much more difficult for money to disappear into the folds of bureaucratic pockets when a blockchain that anyone can see is keeping track of the tab.

*Keeping track of incorporated company details:* The state of Delaware marks the first state in the nation offer incorporated businesses the ability to keep track of their shareholder rights as well as their equity via blockchain. As it is common for many companies to incorporate in Delaware to take advantage of friendly taxation privileges, this has the potential to be a change that has wide-ranging results. The state is also moving its archival records onto a distributed ledger, so that more people can view it, for free, at less cost to taxpayers.

*Digital proof of residency:* In Estonia, long known for its forward-thinking practices, it is now possible to digitally apply for residency in the country through the use of a governmental blockchain. New residents then receive a digital key card that corresponds to a cryptographic key that can be used to sign secure documents, taking the place of any signatures on official paperwork. Virtual residents are then free to open up bank accounts in Estonia's online banking system, which also utilizes blockchain, as well as incorporate a company or access other e-services. Estonia is proud to be pushing the boundaries of digital transactions and seeing a variety of new monetary streams in the process.

*Welfare:* In the United Kingdom, blockchain has already been turned into a service that is available to purchase through the Digital Marketplace run by the government. Through this service, various governmental agencies freely experiment, deploy and build digital services based on blockchain and technology based on distributed ledgers. Last year they ran a trial through the Department for Work and Pension that allowed users to take advantage of a mobile app that let them access their monthly benefit payments along with transferring details to a separate distributed ledger as a means of helping them with managing their finances, with their consent of course.

*Global Blockchain Council:* The Global Blockchain Council has been set up in Dubai and represents more than 50 public and private organizations that have already launched proof-of-concept blockchain projects across the shipping, tourism, digital wills, business registration, title transfer, healthcare records and diamond trading sectors. IBM has also partnered with the organization in hopes of using its blockchain for a logistics and trade solution. The government of Dubai has also announced plans for an initiative to transfer all of their government documents onto an interconnected blockchain by 2020. The estimated cost reduction from this program is anticipated to be at 25.1 million-man hours per year.

# The future of blockchain

While blockchain technology is still in a nascent enough stage that virtually anything can happen, there are a number of things that are being worked on at a governmental level that should be consider in the context of your future usage.

*More control:* As previously mentioned, one of the biggest benefits of a blockchain is its ability to function completely autonomously. However, due to the fact that bitcoin then allowed for near-anonymous transactions, it made it very easy for those with an interest in avoiding the law to do so. As cryptocurrency becomes more well-known, regulatory and governmental agencies including the Securities and Exchange Commission, Department of Homeland Security, FBI, and the Financial Crimes Enforcement Network, just in the US, have all started becoming more interested in its potential for unlawful activities.

Scrutiny began to increase during 2013 when the Financial Crimes Enforcement Network decided that cryptocurrency exchanges represented a form of an existing money service business. This meant that they would then fall under government regulations. DHS quickly took advantage of this fact to freeze the accounts of Mt. Gox, the biggest bitcoin exchange in the world at this time based on accusations of money laundering.

This was then followed up with a more recent SEC ruling to deny bitcoin the ability to open an official cryptocurrency exchange trade fund. This move led to a decrease in the price of bitcoin, though that decrease was then countered by an even stronger increase. The denial of this application was still pending review as of September 2017. This then places cryptocurrencies into a bit of an odd situation as their increasing levels of scrutiny makes it harder for them to follow through on their purpose, despite being more popular than ever.

If cryptocurrency is every going to reach a truly mainstream level, and be absorbed into existing financial systems then it needs to find a way to remain true to its initial purpose while also becoming complex enough to hold off the security threats it is sure to face in the future. What's more, it will also need to become simple enough that the average person can use it without issue. Finally, it would need to remain decentralized enough to still be recognizable, while also including various checks and balances to prevent misuse when it comes to things like money laundering or tax evasion. Taken together, this makes it likely that the successful blockchain of the future is going to be some sort of amalgamation of the current form and a more traditional currency.

*United States:* The United States government is currently working hard to crack down on those who are using blockchain as a means to launder money. They aren't going to be content with that level of control for long, it seems, as signs point to the fact that they are currently working on their own blockchain based cryptocurrency known as Fedcoin. The idea here is that the Federal Reserve could generate a unique cryptocurrency quite easily. The only difference between the blockchain they create and any other is the fact that it would allow for the Federal Reserve to retain the power to go in an remove transactions that they don't approve of.

The rollout of the Fedcoin would occur after the genesis block were created and the rate of Fedcoins being set to 1 to 1 with the dollar. Over time, it would become more and more difficult to come across regular dollars until they were phased out entirely. This would then ultimately lead to a type of cryptocurrency that is both decentralized for its individual transactions, and centralized when it comes to things like limiting available supply and keeping an eye on all types of transactions.

The Federal Reserve is already on its way towards making this plan a reality, so much so that they hosted a closed-door meeting with bitcoin authorities in the fall of 2016. The Chair of the Federal Reserve sat in on the meeting in person, along with representatives from the Bank for International Settlements, World Bank and the International Monetary Fund. During this meeting, one of the talks was literally titled Why Central Banks Will Issue Digital Currencies.

*Russia:* Russia issued a dramatic shift in its cryptocurrency polices in 2017. Prior to this point anyone caught using cryptocurrency could face jail time, now however the country is embracing digital currency wholeheartedly. The reason for this is related to the extreme level of corruption that Russia has seen in its banking sector over the past several years. More than one hundred banks have been closed in the past three years, and a rash of money laundering schemes still can't be stopped.

To better track where its money is going, the Russian government is currently working on several blockchain based technical applications that will make it easier for them to monitor real time transactions. This makes it appear as though they are less interested in creating a new digital currency and are instead more interested in the distributed ledger portion of the blockchain technology. There is currently no word yet on if Russia plans to create a new blockchain or utilize an existing blockchain for its own ends.

*China:* China is currently a major supporter in the blockchain space. In June of 2017, the People's Bank of China released and official news report regarding the creation of its own type of digital currency with the ability to scale dramatically depending on the number of transactions that are seen per day. While all of the details have not yet been released, various sources seem to indicate that the bank could release the currency to the world alongside its renminbi project. While no firm release date is forthcoming, the currency is already well underway in the development process and has already seeing testing amongst many of the country's commercial banks and the People's Bank. This testing is a huge step forward for officially sanctioned cryptocurrencies and blockchains of all types. It also proves how committed China is to the idea of thoroughly exploring the digital currency space.

The digital currency they are creating is likely to cause major gains for their economy overall. This is due to the fact that it is back by the People's Bank which means it is functionally the same as a bank note with far fewer associated fees. It would also do a good deal when it comes to bringing banking in China to the modern age as many of its citizens do not have access to traditional banking services.

# Chapter 3: Cryptocurrency and Blockchain Interactions

While blockchain is poised to do a great many different things in the near future, for now the most important thing you are going to want to keep in mind is that blockchains make cryptocurrency possible, and bitcoin jumped in price more than $2,000 during the summer of 2017. While this price has pushed it out of the league of many amateur investors, there are more than 1,000 different cryptocurrencies on the market these days so there are plenty of opportunities out there for those who are interested in a potentially profitable investment. This is not to say that there isn't risk involved as well, however, so it is important to keep the risks of cryptocurrency investment in mind as well before making any investments in the space.

# Pros

*Lowers risk of identity theft:* As cryptocurrencies are purely digital, they are naturally susceptible to far less risk than traditional types of currency. They cannot be forged or counterfeited and the transaction cannot be manipulated so that it never happened do to the underlying blockchain. Additionally, once you have bought into a cryptocurrency you can move it about freely without have to worry about transactions with specious companies or individuals putting your details in places they would rather not be. Instead, with most exchanges if you already own cryptocurrency there is no type of verification whatsoever. With most exchanges, without cryptocurrency in hand, you need to generate a new debit or credit transaction with each round of funding.

*Easy access:* There are roughly 3.5 billion people who have some type of internet access and also do not have any reliable form of banking. This is a niche that the cryptocurrency market is looking to take advantage of to the fullest, and is expected to cause significant growth in the industry as it becomes more commonplace. Assuming this type of banking catches on, then those who invest in cryptocurrency early are going to see more than just a profit, they could potentially see profit on a significant scale.

*Low cost:* While every cryptocurrency interaction involves a transaction fee, the fees for making this type of exchange is still generally lower than making an exchange on a traditional broker website.

# Cons

*New technology:* While bitcoin has been a quality investment for the past few years, the cryptocurrency market as a whole is still extremely untested overall which means that many of its risks are still very poorly defined, especially when compared to more traditional markets. This naturally makes the highs in the market more dramatic than similar markets, but it also makes the lowers much more dramatic as well. There are no guarantees when one is going to become the other, trends can come and go in completely unpredictable patterns that no one has seen before. What it all comes down to is that there just is not enough information available to be able to accurately predict where the market is going to be in a year, much less five. Until the market stabilizes somewhat, there is no way of telling if every dollar you invest is going to be worth $2, one year from now or if it is going to be worth $.02.

*Extreme volatility:* Bitcoin, the most stable of all of the cryptocurrencies, is still five time more volatile than gold and has nearly seven times more volatility than if you were to invest that money into the S&P 500. While volatility means a greater chance at profit, it also means the chance at a loss is going to be much higher than it would otherwise be. It is also important to understand that most of the purchases of cryptocurrency that are made, are done for speculative purposes. This means that the currency is being purchased by investors, not people who are actually planning to use it on a day-to-day basis. This, in turn means that prices are likely to rise higher than a true supply and demand market would indicate. This early adopter phenomenon means those who buy in early are going to experience a nice price increase, but the upward movement ultimately won't last. This isn't a question of if, it is a question of when.

*Lack of physicality:* While the fact that cryptocurrency is a digital means of payment is one of its leading characteristics, the fact remains that this concept does present some challenges. Specifically, consider the fact that if the server holding your cryptocurrency goes down, and there is no backup, then your investment is gone forever. You can take a variety of methods to put the control of your cryptocurrency in your hands, but the fact remains that a real coin is always going to be easier to hold onto than a digital one.

The vast potential for profit when it comes to hacking into a blockchain also means that hackers are never going to stop trying to do just that. What this also means, is that they are occasionally going to be successful. For example, the Ethereum platform has seen a variety of different attacks throughout its lifetime, one of which was so successful that it necessitated a hard fork that saw the Ethereum blockchain divided into those that saw a profit from the attack and those who lost out because of it. A split in the value of the dollar is never going to occur, no matter how many are stolen in a bank robbery which just proves how unpredictable investing in a new opportunity can be.

## Trading cryptocurrency

Regardless of how familiar you are with trading traditional securities, trading in the cryptocurrency market can prove to be extremely profitable, as long as you have come to terms with the potential for risk. Don't forget, it is important to never invest any money that you can't afford to lose. There is very little barrier to entry, as previously mentioned, if you already have cryptocurrency then you won't even need to worry about verifying your account.

Another useful thing about trading in this market is the fact that there are no centralized exchanges which means it is every exchange for itself. This then leads to a market that is very fragmented, which means it naturally produces spreads that are much wider than you are likely to see anywhere else. This lack of regulation also means it is often quite easy to find a very large margin which means that small investments have the potential to become large returns faster than with virtually all other types of investment, though the same can be said about losses as well. Finally, depending on the cryptocurrency you are trading in, you will likely be able to find it for different rates on different exchanges which means you might be able to make a profit simply by purchasing them in one place and selling them somewhere else.

The most common way to trade cryptocurrencies through a trading company is with a contract for differences. This type of contract binds the buyer and seller together for the length of the contract, once it ends, the buyer will pay the seller the difference between the price of the asset at the end of the contract and what it was at the start. If the price moves the other way then the seller has to pay the buyer the difference. When it comes to securing leverage, you will likely be able to find rates in excess of 20 to 1, though it is not recommended that you seek them out until you are very familiar with what it is like to trade in this market.

*Global currency:* When it comes to standard currency, the number of things that can influence the price is naturally going to be fairly limited. The opposite is true for cryptocurrencies, however, and it is difficult to tell what is going to set investors off before it happens. Any currency news anywhere has the potential to set prices shifting dramatically, in fact, several of bitcoin's most significant moves have come about due to the introduction to controls for capital in Greece and when China devalued the Yuan.

*Market always ready:* While the forex market is traditionally thought of as the most robust market as it is open 120 hours each week, the cryptocurrency market is open 168 hours each week, and trades are always happening regardless of what part of the world is currently active. Currently there are about 100 major cryptocurrency exchanges in the world who all offer various levels of trading along with differing rates based on their level of service. As such, it should not take more than a little research to find the one that is right for you.

This can also be seen as a negative, depending on your tolerance for risk as these factors can be enough to generate large swings on a daily basis. In fact, price shifts of more than 5 percent are common on most days for the larger cryptocurrencies and the smaller ones aren't surprised if they see 15 percent movement or more.

# Finding your exchange

When it comes to committing to a specific exchange, it is important to always do the relevant research that you need in order to feel comfortable about your choice. Moving forward without doing enough research can cause you to end up in a situation where you exchange suddenly disappears with your money or you find out that it doesn't have the funds to cover all of its obligations and there is a run on it as everyone tries to get their money back at once. If this sort of thing were to happen, it is important to keep in mind that you are going to have very little recourse, especially if you choose an exchange that is not based in your country. This is why the initial choice you make has the potential to be so impactful.

*Prioritize transparent exchanges:* As a general rule, the more transparent the exchange you choose is willing to be, the more on the level it is going to be. This means you are going to want to be able to take a look at their order book, which is just a version of their distributed ledger and shows how much of everything is being bought or sold on a regular basis. You should also be able to request details regarding where their funds are held and their system for verifying their appropriate level of reserve currency. If you have a hard time getting answers to these very basic questions then the exchange might simply not have the means to make that information public. On the other hand, it could mean that they are a fractional exchange and can't cover their debts. When it comes to choosing the right cryptocurrency exchange it is always better to be safe than sorry.

*Available security:* It is very important to always choose an exchange with a healthy level of security, after all, as previously mentioned your cryptocurrency profits won't exist outside this exchange without your help which means security is of the upmost importance. You will only want to use exchanges that have an HTTPS in front of their URL as this indicates they are operating off of a secure protocol which means they are actively working to keep your account details from being stolen. You will also want to ensure that the exchange is utilizing a type of two-factor authentication in addition to standard secure login practices. If your exchange isn't at least this well protected then you are flirting with theft of both your identity and your investments.

*Fees add up:* Almost every type of cryptocurrency has an associated fee that is paid, part of which goes to the blockchain platform holder and part goes to the miner or miners who verify your transaction. While these fees are certainly voluntary, in most cases, not paying them removes much of the incentive for your transaction to be verified which means the entire process might end up taking longer than it otherwise would. Unless you choose an exchange in China, you will then also have to pay a transaction fee to the exchange as well. With so many fees flying around, they can add up quickly which means you are always going to have a trading plan in place before you make your first trade to prevent yourself from losing a sizeable portion of your trading capital to fees.

*Try for something local:* Despite the fact that there are cryptocurrency exchanges worldwide, you should aim for one that operates in your home country if possible. This is advantageous in multiple ways, the first of which is that you will naturally be able to take advantage of periods of higher volume simply because you will be on the same general time zone as your exchange. Choosing a local option will also make it easier should you ever need to contact support, and your deposits will go through more quickly as well. Even better, depending on your country and its laws, there might even be some type of oversight regarding cryptocurrency exchanges which means getting your money back after some funny business might not be completely out of the question.

When choosing a local exchange, make sure to verify they offer the cryptocurrency pairs that you are looking for. Exchanges vary dramatically from one to the next so there are no guarantees you will even be able to trade in your local currency, even if you pick an exchange that is close to home.

*Understand transaction times:* As all cryptocurrency transaction need to be verified and added to the blockchain before they can clear, exchanges often work on a bit of a lead time to let this process breathe. It is important that you choose an exchange whose transaction time is reasonable, for the best results. Likewise, you are going to want to ensure that the price you buy at is the price that is locked in regardless of how long the transaction takes. If this is not the case then you risk making a trade that looks promising, only to have the price change and ruin everything before it actually goes through.

# Well-known exchanges

*Kraken:* This is a European exchange that handles the highest volume of euro trades each day. They are also within the top 15 when it comes to USD exchanges as well.

*Coinbase:* This is the elder statesman of the cryptocurrency exchanges in the US and has the honor of being the oldest continuously active USD exchange. It is known for being strictly regulated and is still one of the top five when it comes to pure volume traded per day.

**If you sign up for Coinbase using this link, you will receive $10 worth of free Bitcoin after your first purchase of more than $100 worth of cryptocurrency.**

http://bit.ly/10dollarbtc

*OKCoin:* This is primarily a USD exchange that is based in Japan which means it is subject to far fewer regulations than most of the other exchanges in this list. If you are looking for higher margins and few fees, and are comfortable with the extra risk, then this is the exchange for you.

*Bitstamp:* This exchange has been running continuously since 2011 and the second most commonly used USD exchange with a volume greater than 10,000 units a day.

*Bitfinex:* This exchange does the greatest amount of USD trading by volume of all the exchanges, worldwide, clearing more than 200,000 units of cryptocurrency every single week. If you are interested in going with this option, be aware that if you already own cryptocurrency then you can get started without submitting to any type of verification.

# Initial coin offerings (ICOs)

In 2017, a blockchain based company managed
to raise more than $150 million in less than 24
hours and another, Status.im managed half that
amount. These outpourings of investor
generosity are known as initial coin offerings
and, like everything having to do with
cryptocurrency, they offer a heavy risk in
exchange for a potentially lucrative reward. As of
summer, 2017, the process had already raised
nearly $500,000,000.

Despite being a play on the term initial public
offering, the initial coin offering is actually a very
different beast in almost every way. An initial
coin offering is really just another crowdfunding
strategy where a blockchain company offers its
new cryptocurrency at a very investor-friendly
rate and then investors buy it up in hopes of
seeing the price rise even as little as 50 cents.
The company then, in theory at least, will have

the money to complete its project and come to market, where its products or services will be so widely adopted that the price of its cryptocurrency will rise based on increased demand. The Ethereum platform has quickly proven itself the most popular home for companies who are looking to offer an initial coin offering.

A majority of this money currently comes from China, though investors from around the world have been known to open their checkbooks if the price is right. While investing on what is more or less an unknown quantity always comes with certain risks, initial coin offerings are even riskier still. This is due to the fact that they are not currently under the SEC regulatory umbrella which means their business plans are not put through the same testing that those who apply for an initial public offering are. There is also some concern that the success that the first few initial coin offerings garnered is actually due to another bubble which means it is unlikely to last.

While they do have issues, initial coin offerings also have the potential to generate serious profits for investors who make the right decisions at the right times. Nevertheless, if you are considering this type of investment then you need to understand that if you choose to invest in an initial coin offering, then you are making one of the riskiest investments possible.

To counteract the potential danger as much as possible, you will need to approach all initial coin offerings with a quizzical mindset and the first thing you will want to do is look through any information the company has made available including, hopefully, a business plan. This will make it easier for you to determine if a specific project makes sense on a financial level and to ensure that is business proposition checks out in the long-term. You will also need to know that the market is going to actually want the product or service the company is hoping to provide. Furthermore, you will want to double check and see what the role of the cryptocurrency that you are buying into will be when the product or service is up and running.

You will also need to keep in mind that buying into an initial coin offering is going to be quite different than buying into an initial public offering. When buying into the latter, you come away with ownership shares that essentially mean you own a small portion of the company in question. Initial coin offerings grant you no such rights, just a pile of digital currency that may or may not eventually be worth something. Additionally, initial public offerings have stricter requirements placed on them including accreditation obligations and fiduciary requirements that the company must meet before it can have its offering, none of which is required for initial coin offerings.

In reality, you are likely never going to see more than a whitepaper, business plan and website from an initial coin offering company, and sometimes not even all of these. They are more than likely not going to have a product or prototype to show off either which means you are going to be taking a lot of what is being told to you on faith. You also need to be aware that just because an initial coin offering sees a good amount of response early on, doesn't mean this goodwill will last until its launch day, much less beyond it. Also noteworthy is the fact that many analysts believe that giving new companies too much money too soon actually limits their potential as the owner's feel the need to spend all the money available to them while feeling less inclined to actually complete a usable product.

While the list of poor ICOs ranges from those with overly optimistic ideas to downright scams with the sole goal of taking your hard earned cash. There are an increasing number of ICOs out there with nothing more than a flashy website filled with a ton of buzzwords and a high valuation based on nothing more than their own opinion. The single biggest factor you should examine before investing is the real world viability of the project. What solution to a current problem does the company promise to solve? Even more so, is there even a problem in the first place that requires blockchain technology? It's important to examine the team behind the project, and more importantly their previous track record with projects like it. Another main determinant should be whether the token they are offering has actual utility for the project, or are investors just going to dump it for a quick profit as soon as it hits the open market? You should also watch out for any huge bonuses offered for early investors. It's not uncommon for a pre-sale bonus to be offered, but if these bonuses top 100%, you can and should question what the incentive is for non-early adopters, and if the team are just trying to generate as much cash as quickly as possible. One advantage the Ethereum platform does have is the ability for smart contracts to be coded into the ICO, such as funds held in a service similar to escrow, to ensure they are returned to investors if the project founders do not uphold their end of the agreement.

Last but not least, it is worth noting that a majority of the currently successful initial coin offerings have been based on the Ethereum blockchain platform which means the basis of these companies is still essentially an untested technology. While the Ethereum blockchain platform has a better chance of making it than making it than most, the fact of the matter is that it is still untested technology so there is still downside potential as well as upside. Overall, it might be the best choice to instead wait and see how the first round of initial coin offering companies pan out before getting too involved with these types of investments directly.

# Tips for investing successfully

While starting to invest in cryptocurrency is as easy as finding an exchange and putting some money into the cryptocurrency machine, doing so and turning an investment profit is something else completely. What's next is a list of things you will want to keep in mind in order to invest successfully in the long-term.

*It's a commodity:* The first thing you are going to need to do is to think about cryptocurrency in the same way you would any other commodity. Just like any other commodity, cryptocurrency is used for practical as well as investment purposes, just as precious metals have commercial uses and base metals have industrial ones. Additionally, they are all trade through exchanges that more or less all follow the same rules. This means that in order to choose a cryptocurrency that is likely to increase in value, you are going to want to pick the one that is likely to provide the most real-world value or has the greatest number of probable uses beyond just P2P transactions.

*Increasing usage:* When gathered together as a whole, all the currently existing cryptocurrencies have a market cap of about $160 billion. This puts them in the same league as companies like Tesla and Microsoft in terms of pure numbers. What makes this number particularly interesting is that real world usage and increasing market cap have gone hand in hand so far, and reports show that blockchain and cryptocurrency usage is only likely to increase for at least the next five years.

This is when market saturation is expected to occur and is likely when many of the existing bubbles break for the first time. Nevertheless, while the market is still extremely volatile in the short-term, cryptocurrency as a long-term investment should be relatively reliable. When this number is looked at through the lens of the current market cap then the potential for growth is truly staggering. Essentially the price of cryptocurrency across the board has nowhere to go but up. Even better, once the number of users eventually stabilizes, investor won't have to worry about the bubble effect nearly as much because prices will likely stop decreasing dramatically at that point as well.

*Point in the cycle:* The market cycle is a type of investment pattern that every investment goes through sooner or later. On the positive side, it starts with optimism before moving up to thrill, and then peaking with euphoria. It then decreases through anxiety, denial, fear, depression and finally, panic. After it bottoms out it then rises back up through depression, hope and relief before once again reaching optimism.

While bitcoin has already been through the cycle more than once, most recently bottoming out during the 2014 crash, the vast majority of all cryptocurrencies are still very much in the optimism stage so there is still plenty of time to get in while the getting is good. As long as you do your research correctly in the first place there is no reason you couldn't realistically see five reliable years of growth on your investment before it hits the euphoria stage.

While this is decidedly good news, it is also important to keep in mind the fact that the cryptocurrency market today, is very much the same as the dotcom boom of the 90s. What this means, is that roughly 80 percent of all the cryptocurrencies on the market today are going to fail before or during the period when the market hits its saturation point. This is due to the fact that there will only be so many options in a limited marketplace that only a handful will be able to survive the buildup. Many investors will end up throwing their money at a company without having any idea what that company actually does and the market will crumble because of it, though if you know what's coming you will be able to avoid the worst of it.

*Solving problems is key:* It doesn't matter what the potential for profit on a given cryptocurrency turns out to be, buying into it and then sitting back to wait for the magic to happen will never be the most effective money-making strategy. Instead, you will be better served putting time into finding those cryptocurrencies that solve problems for individual markets or, even better, the world at large. The bigger the problem being solved, the more likely it will turn into something that is worth investing in for the long-term. It is especially important to consider solutions when it comes to the banking services that some parts of the world take for granted. Cryptocurrencies that focus on solutions when it comes to making payments and wiring money are going to be good bets in the near future.

*Long-term view:* Given the amount of movement you can expect to see on a regular basis, the ideal cryptocurrency portfolio is going to be one that focuses solely on the long-term. You are also going to want to make a point of picking several different cryptocurrencies to invest in, between three or five, so that you will never be too negatively affected by serious drops in one place or another. More than anything else it is going to be important that you control your emotions as thoroughly as possible and strive to avoid rash decisions when investments are on the line. When you are first getting started it is a good idea to not watch your investments too closely, as they are likely going to be all over the place. Don't forget, the goal to long-term investing is a steady overall upward trend which means a little back and forth is to be expected.

It is also important to remember that cryptocurrencies do not come with the lock-in risk that many other long-term investments do. If you feel that a certain cryptocurrency's time has come, you can quickly and easily exchange it with any other currency you choose, instead of having to go through the hassle of trading in a more traditional fashion during a down market. As such, you may want to think about investing in cryptocurrency as just keeping money in a savings account, but one that has a much higher potential for return on your primary investment.

# Conclusion

Thank you for making it through to the end of *Blockchain Beginners Bible: Discover How Blockchain Could Influence Your Business*, let's hope it was informative and able to provide you with all of the tools you need to achieve your goals, whatever it is that they may be. Just because you've finished this book doesn't mean there is nothing left to learn on the topic, expanding your horizons is the only way to find the mastery you seek.

This is especially true for the blockchain market as it is a new enough technology as to literally be always changing. Only by making it a habit to become a lifelong learner will you ever truly get a grasp on it that you will be able to use for your advantage. Whatever you do, always keep in mind that the market is heading towards an inevitable saturation point which means however you decide to interact with blockchain technology you need to ensure you end up on the right side of it.

It is extremely likely that you will not see another technology this disruptive in your lifetime, and with so many technology variations and cryptocurrencies all vying for the market at once, all you need to do is be aware of the possibility of success to be able to seek it out and reap all the related rewards. It also means that there are plenty of ways to fail, however, so you are going to really need to do your homework and ensure that you never make a move without taking all of your options into consideration fist. Remember, investing in blockchain technology is investing in the long-term, slow and steady wins the race.

Finally, if you found this book useful in anyway, a review on Amazon is always appreciated!